MY FIRST BABY SIGNS

OVER 40 FUNDAMENTAL SIGNS FOR YOU AND BABY

LEE ANN STEYNS

ILLUSTRATED BY JULIA SEAL

 PETER PAUPER PRESS, INC.
Rye Brook, New York

To my original signing babies, Ella and Ian,
and my biggest supporter, Scott

PETER PAUPER PRESS

In 1928, at the age of twenty-two, Peter Beilenson began printing books on a small press in the basement of his parents' home in Larchmont, New York. Peter—and later, his wife, Edna—sought to create fine books that sold at "prices even a pauper could afford."

Today, still family owned and operated, Peter Pauper Press continues to honor our founders' legacy of quality, value, and fun for big kids and small kids alike.

Note: Variations of signs are common. The signs in this book represent ones used most commonly in baby sign language.

Designed by Heather Zschock
Text copyright © 2023 Lee Ann Steyns
Illustrations copyright © 2023 Julia Seal
All rights reserved. No part of this book may be used or reproduced in any manner whatsoever without written permission from the publisher.

Published by Peter Pauper Press, Inc.
3 International Drive
Rye Brook, NY 10573 USA

Published in the United Kingdom and Europe by Peter Pauper Press, Inc.
c/o White Pebble International,
Units 2-3, Spring Business Park,
Stanbridge Road, Havant, Hampshire PO9 2GJ, UK

Library of Congress Control Number: 2023028168

ISBN 978-1-4413-4004-7

Printed in China

7 6 5 4 3 2 1

Visit us at www.peterpauper.com

INTRODUCTION

Your baby has so much to tell you!

Before my young daughter could talk at all, she was a fussy, colicky baby—and I was a tired, frustrated mom who desperately wanted to know how to help her feel better. Finding a way to communicate became my first objective and I soon learned that signing worked. Using a few simple signs with my 6-month-old daughter created a complete shift in our days, and within a few months she was able to understand and sign back over fifteen signs for clear communication at mealtime, playtime, and bedtime—we kept adding signs and never looked back.

Learning simple signs together with your baby is a game changer. It encourages your baby to communicate and improves your ability to understand them. It can help cut down on frustration-related crying and fussing as you're both able to use signs to communicate with each other.

I've designed My First Baby Signs to steadily introduce helpful American Sign Language (ASL), so you'll see exactly what to sign and how to start signing. The picture-book format keeps the learning fun while introducing baby signs in context—pairing them with easy-to-follow visual and written guides on how to do each sign. The story gently follows a baby's day from sunup to sundown while showcasing different families throughout.

Begin with the Top 10 Starter Signs that are suited to life with a baby, then build up to adding over thirty more Daily Signs for your routines and activities at your own pace. Babies can start to comprehend signs as early as 2–3 months old or any time after, and can typically start performing signs themselves to communicate back around 8–14 months old. This is an estimation, since each baby is different.

This book reflects the curriculum I've been teaching families for over fifteen years and holds the signs and strategies for your family to become a successful signing family, too.

TOP 10 STARTER SIGNS

The first ten signs will allow your baby to express basic needs and wants with simple gestures that they will be motivated to learn because they're easy and fun! Begin by picking one or two signs, using them as you introduce an activity. Slowly build more signs in as you feel ready.

- You can use either hand to sign one-handed signs, but you may have a dominant hand that feels more natural to use.

- Always say the word out loud that you are signing so your baby gets to hear and see what you're saying. This deepens how they can absorb language and begin understanding what your words mean.

- It's best to say and sign what's about to happen next. For instance, you can say, "It's time for MILK, here's your MILK, we're having MILK now" as you hand them a bottle or begin feeding. This creates context so baby can start connecting both the word and sign with what happens when you present it.

- Try to sign while your baby can see your hands and your face, but don't worry if they're not looking directly at you–sign anyway! Your little one will notice that you are consistently presenting signs alongside speaking and will be inspired to learn the signs with you. It will also allow you to practice your signs and feel more confident.

HAVE FUN! We all learn better when we are enjoying ourselves, and reading this story together is a perfect signing experience to keep things playful.

MILK

Baby is having some milk.

Open and close your fist twice
like squeezing.

ALL DONE

Soon Baby's all done
and ready for a burp.

Hold up both hands with
palms facing you, then twist
so palms face out.

UP

Dad picks up Baby and gives them a pat, pat, pat.

Point up with an extended index finger.

CHANGE

Then it's time to change Baby.

Tap both closed fists on top of each other with index fingers extended into a hook, then turn over to tap again with the other fist on top.

DIAPER

Silly Baby!
That's not where
a diaper goes!

Hold both hands at the waist
and tap the index and middle
fingers to the thumbs twice.

9

PLAY

Mommy gives Baby something else to play with. It's a ball!

With palms facing in and thumbs and pinky fingers extended, shake hands outward twice.

MORE

And there are more toys
for Baby in here.

Tap both hands with the
fingertips connected to the thumbs
in front of the body a few times.

11

BATH

Bath time is full of bubbly fun.

Rub both closed fists up and down the chest twice.

MOMMY

Mommy wraps up Baby
in a soft towel.

Tap the extended thumb of an
open flat hand to the chin.

DADDY

Daddy helps
Baby get dressed.

Tap the extended thumb of an
open flat hand to the forehead.

DAILY SIGNS

These next signs allow you to build more complex communication with your baby around daily activities like eating, playing, going outside, bathing, and bedtime.

WHAT TO EXPECT:
The 4 Stages of Learning Signs for Babies

Parents in my baby sign classes are always curious to see the end result of their baby signing back when I start teaching signs to them and their little ones. But it's very important to see each stage of learning unfold at your baby's pace and keep building and learning signs together. Here are the stages:

1. ### Reception
   Babies need to watch us and take in what we show them, no matter their age, stage, or ability. Don't let them fool you into thinking they're not paying attention; babies take in everything.

2. ### Response
   Babies will begin to understand what's happening as we present signs alongside our daily activities, and they will respond. This could be a big smile when you sign "eat" if they're hungry, or reaching for their pet when you sign "cat." My daughter, Ella, would almost take flight by flapping her arms in excitement when I signed MILK before feeding.

3. ### Mimicking
   Next, babies will start making attempts to mimic back what they see their parents doing. This will most likely look clumsy at first.

4. ### Signing
   Once baby has reached the developmental stage of being able to move their hands independently, their signs will slowly start taking shape. Their "babbling" hands will develop and become more intentional as they gain more dexterity.

EAT

Time to eat, yum!

Move one hand with fingertips connected to thumb toward the mouth twice.

16

Baby is going to have cereal.

Move index finger sideways across lips, curling and straightening as it moves.

BANANA

And some banana, too.

Pretend your index finger is
a banana and peel it open with
your other hand.

WATER

Baby drinks water, slurp, slurp, slurp.

Tap the index finger of a "W" hand to the mouth twice.

CLEAN

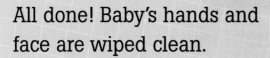

All done! Baby's hands and
face are wiped clean.

Stack both hands flat with
palms facing each other and slide
one hand across the other
toward the fingertips.

PLEASE

Baby says "Please" to get out of the high chair.

Make a circular motion with your open flat hand on the top of your chest.

HELP

Baby asks Mommy for help to get up, up, up into her arms.

Make a thumbs-up fist. Place it on the palm of your other hand and move both hands upward.

THANK YOU

"Thank you," Mommy!

Move your flat hand in an arc from lips out toward the person you are thanking.

READY

Everyone's ready
to go outside.

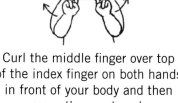

Curl the middle finger over top
of the index finger on both hands
in front of your body and then
move them outward.

SHOES

Mommy helps put
Baby's shoes on.

Tap the sides of both of your
closed fists together twice.

25

HAT

And a hat on Baby's head.

Pat the top of your head with a flat hand twice.

DOG

Look who's going out, too!
It's Pepper the dog!

Snap your fingers using your
middle finger twice.

27

CAT

Baby sees a cat
in the window.

Pinch your thumb and index finger
together and move from your cheek
outward as if showing whiskers.

FRIEND

Baby meets a friend
at the park.

Interlock curved index
fingers together with one
on top, then switch.

COLD

Baby's hands feel cold
on this windy day.

Hunch your shoulders and
wiggle your fists.

BLANKET

Daddy pulls up the blanket to keep Baby warm.

Pretend to pull a blanket up to your neck with the thumbs under the fingers.

HOME

Everyone's back
at home now.

Bring fingers and thumb
together to touch cheek and then
touch in front of ear.

TOY

Baby is building a tower of toy blocks.

Twist your wrists with both hands closed in a fist with thumbs up between the index and middle fingers.

GENTLE

Baby is gentle with
Pepper the dog.

Make a fist with one hand
and gently stroke it with
the other hand.

POTTY

Baby needs to use
the potty.

Make a fist with the thumb
up between the middle and
index finger and shake it
from side to side twice.

WASH HANDS

Time to wash hands after Baby uses the potty.

Rub and twist both hands over each other as if washing your hands.

HOT

Daddy makes sure the water is not too hot.

Move your open claw hand starting at mouth quickly down and away from the body.

37

TOWEL

Dad has a nice clean towel to dry Baby's hands.

Hold both hands above your shoulders and move them side to side as if you are drying your back.

GRANDMA

Baby sees Grandma coming through the front door.

With an open hand and thumb at chin, move your hand forward in an arc and then a second arc.

39

GRANDPA

Grandpa has come to visit Baby, too.

With an open hand and thumb at forehead, move your hand forward in an arc and then a second arc.

LOVE

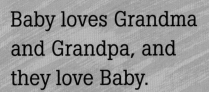

Baby loves Grandma
and Grandpa, and
they love Baby.

Cross your arms with closed
fists over your chest.

BED

Baby is sleepy.
It's time for bed.

Put flat hands together, palm to palm, at the side of your head and rest your head on your hands.

BOOK

Daddy reads Baby
a bedtime book.

Connect both flat hands
together, then open your hands
as if opening a book.

SONG

They sing a song to say goodnight, la la la.

Extend your forearm with palm up and sway your other hand back and forth over it.

Baby gets
a kiss from
Mommy and
Daddy, mwah!

Tap your hands together once
with fingertips connected to
thumbs and pucker your lips.

45

LIGHTS

Daddy turns out the lights for bedtime.

Hold both hands above your head with your fingertips together, then spread open your fingers twice.

Mommy and Daddy say
I LOVE YOU to Baby.

Hold up one hand with index
finger, pinky finger, and thumb
extended, palm facing out.

INDEX OF SIGNS

All Done, 6
Banana, 18
Bath, 12
Bed, 42
Blanket, 31
Book, 43
Cat, 28
Cereal, 17
Change, 8
Clean, 20
Cold, 30
Daddy, 14
Diaper, 9
Dog, 27
Eat, 16
Friend, 29
Gentle, 34
Grandma, 39
Grandpa, 40
Hat, 26
Help, 22
Home, 32
Hot, 37
I Love You, 47
Kiss, 45

Lights, 46
Love, 41
Milk, 5
Mommy, 13
More, 11
Play, 10
Please, 21
Potty, 35
Ready, 24
Shoes, 25
Song, 44
Thank You, 23
Towel, 38
Toy, 33
Up, 7
Wash Hands, 36
Water, 19

BATH

KISS

HELP

THANK YOU